Friendship with *Jesus*

Pope Benedict XVI Speaks to Children on their First Holy Communion

Amy Welborn, *Editor*

Ann Kissane Engelhart, *Illustrator*

MAGNIFICAT · Ignatius

Original UK edition: The Incorporated Catholic Truth Society, 40–46 Harleyford Road, London SE11 5AY. www.cts-online.uk.

ISBN Ignatius: 978-1-58617-619-8
ISBN Magnificat: 978-1-936260-42-3
Printed by Tien Wah Press, Malaysia
Printed on September, 2013
Job Number MGN 13016-02
Printed in Malaysia in compliance with the Consumer Protection Safety Act, 2008.

Contents

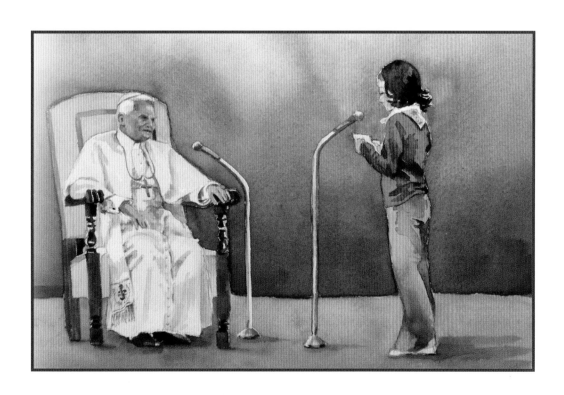

One sunny afternoon, a number of children went to visit Pope Benedict XVI in Rome.

Hundreds came, with their moms and dads, sisters, brothers and grandparents.

They took buses and the subway. They walked down the narrow winding streets of Rome to the Vatican, where the Holy Father lives. Talking, laughing and singing, they went to the great piazza in front of St Peter's Basilica.

And it was just here in the piazza—so close to where the first Pope, St Peter, had given his life for Jesus, that the children waited. They had all received their First Holy Communion during the year. They had come to celebrate with the Holy Father, who walks in St Peter's footsteps today.

It was a great day! Pope Benedict, dressed in the white robes that the Pope always wears, came to spend time with the children. They prayed and sang together. They did something else, too:

They talked!

The children had questions for the Holy Father. They wanted to know about his First Communion. They wanted to know more about how Jesus comes to them in Communion. They had a lot of good questions.

So several of the children sat with the Holy Father, and they started to have a conversation.

__Andrea__ received his First Holy Communion not so long ago. Pope Benedict was once a little child too, so Andrea asked:

"**"Dear Pope, what are your memories of your First Communion day?"**"

It was a lovely Sunday in March 1936, sixty-nine years ago. It was a sunny day; the church looked very beautiful; there was music… There were so many beautiful things that I remember. There were about thirty of us, boys and girls from my little village of no more than 500 inhabitants.

But at the heart of my joyful and beautiful memories is this one… I understood that Jesus had entered my heart; he had actually visited me. And with Jesus, God himself was with me. And I realized that this is a gift of love that is truly worth more than all the other things that life can give.

__What do you think you will remember about your First Communion day?__

'Then they told their story of what had happened on the road,
and how they had recognized him at the breaking of bread.' (Luke 24:35)

Livia *asked:*

"Holy Father, before the day of my First Holy Communion I went to confession. I have also been to confession on other occasions. I wanted to ask you: do I have to go to confession every time I receive Communion, even when I have committed the same sins? Because I realize that they are always the same."

Our sins are always the same—but we clean our homes, our rooms, at least once a week, even if the dirt is always the same; this helps us to live in cleanliness and to start again. Otherwise, we might not see the dirt building up.

Something similar can be said about the soul. Take me for example: if I never go to confession, my soul is neglected and in the end I am always pleased with myself. Then I no longer understand that I must always work hard to improve and that I must make progress.

How do you feel after your sins are forgiven in Confession?

Andrea *asked:*

"**In preparing me for my First Holy Communion day, my catechist told me that Jesus is present in the Eucharist. But how? I can't see him!**"

No, we cannot see him, but there are many things that we do not see but they exist and are essential… We don't see an electric current, for example, yet we see that it exists; we see this microphone, that it is working, and we see lights. Therefore, even if we do not see the very deepest things, those that really sustain life and the world, we can still see and feel their effects. This is also true for electricity; we do not see the electric current but we see the light.

So it is with the Risen Lord: we do not see him with our eyes but we see that wherever Jesus is, people change, they improve…

Therefore, even if we do not see the Lord himself we still see the effects of the Lord: so we can understand that Jesus is present. And as I said, it is precisely the invisible things that are the most profound, the most important. So let us go to meet this invisible but powerful Lord who helps us to live well.

What do you say to Jesus when you receive him in Holy Communion?

Giulia asked:

"Your Holiness, everyone tells us that it is important to go to Mass on Sunday. We would gladly go, but often our parents do not take us because on Sundays they sleep. The parents of a friend of mine work in a shop, and in my family we often go to the country to visit our grandparents. Could you say something to them, to make them understand that it is important to go to Mass together on Sundays?"

I would think so, of course, with great love and great respect for your parents, because they certainly have a lot to do. However, with a daughter's respect and love, you could say to them: "Dear Mommy, dear Daddy, it is so important for us all, even for you, to meet Jesus. Meeting Jesus enriches us. It is an important part of our lives. Let's find a little time together; we can find a way."

How can you help your family to enjoy meeting Jesus in the Eucharist at Mass?

'Let the little children come to me, and do not stop them; for it is to such as these that the kingdom of God belongs.' (Luke 18:16)

'Jesus Christ is Lord!' (Philippians 2:11)

Alessandro *asked:*

> "What good does it do in our everyday life to go to Holy Mass and receive Communion?"

It centers life. We live amid so many things. And the people who do not go to church do not know that it is precisely Jesus they lack. But they feel that something is missing in their lives. If God is absent from my life, if Jesus is absent from my life, then a guide, an essential friend is missing; a great joy is missing from my life as well, the strength to grow as a man, to overcome my vices and to mature as a human being.

How does Jesus' friendship help you every day?

Anna asked:

"**"Dear Holy Father, can you explain to us what Jesus meant when he said to the people who were following him: 'I am the bread of life?'"**"

When Jesus says, "I am the bread of life", it means that Jesus himself is the nourishment we need for our soul, for our inner self, because the soul also needs food. We really need God's friendship, which helps us to make the right decisions. We need to mature as human beings. In other words: Jesus nourishes us so that we can truly become mature people and our lives become good.

In what part of your life do you need the special nourishment of Jesus, the Bread of Life?

'I am the bread of life. Whoever comes to me will never be hungry, and whoever believes in me will never be thirsty.' (John 6:35)

When the children and the Holy Father had finished talking, Eucharistic Adoration began.

Before that **Adriano** *asked:*

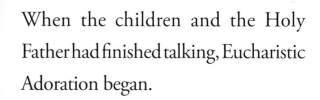

"Holy Father, they've told us that today we will have Eucharistic Adoration. What is it? How is it done? Can you explain it to us?"

Adoration is recognizing that Jesus is my Lord, and that Jesus shows me the way to take. It helps me to see that I will live well only if I know the road that Jesus points out and I follow the path he shows me…

Adoration means saying: "Jesus, I am yours. I will follow you in my life. I never want to lose this friendship, this communion with you." I could also say that adoration is essentially an embrace with Jesus in which I say to him: "I am yours, and, I ask you, please stay with me always".

If you were going to pray to Jesus right now in Eucharistic Adoration, for what would you thank him?

'And remember, I am with you always,
to the end of the age.' (Matthew 28:20)

'Peace be with you. As the Father has sent me, so I send you.' (John 20:21)

It had been a wonderful conversation! The children had asked very good questions. Now it was time for Eucharistic Adoration and then, after that, time to take the Good News of Jesus' love out into the world. The Holy Father had some special words of farewell:

At the end of our meeting, I repeat the words from the beginning of every liturgy. I say to you: "Peace be with you"; that is, may the Lord be with you, may joy be with you, and so may your lives be good.

Have a good Sunday; good night and I hope to see you again soon all together with the Lord.